Amazon Echo Show

Everything You Should Know About Amazon Echo Show From Beginner To Advanced

Introduction

The Amazon Echo Show is the next upgrade for Alexa – you'll hear a lot of people saying it's Alexa with a screen. That being said, you can say that this is a visual upgrade so to speak. Now Alexa can provide you with some visuals. Of course, if you're a fan of the Echo and other previous products in this line, you may have already figured out that there are controls and commands that are easier to access with something visual or on-screen, right?

And that is what the Echo Show gives you and more. Some have said that the experience with this "version" of Alexa is that you now let her see you and you in a way see her. So what should you expect from this device? Here's a little sneak peak:

- For one thing it is easy to use
- There are features from Alexa that are definitely a lot better with some visual displays such as lists and timers for instance.
- It can play video. Now, that's something you can't do with a smart speaker.
- You also get visual search results

Are there things that the boys from the Amazon think tank should improve on? The answer is yes. Note that the Echo Show has tons of potential, which is why the competition is hard at work trying to match it. However, here are a few downsides that everyone should know about:

- It has no privacy shutter – that means people can Drop on you and of course you can't deny access to the person calling (aka see what you're up to at the moment when they start the video conference)

- Some of the skills that come with this Show are good but there are a few kinks that do need some work.

We all know that Amazon's smart digital assistant is always improving and the Echo Show is proof of that. Here in this book we'll cover everything you need to know about it and we're unabashedly going to include both what's to like about it and what not.

After reading through this book you will know how to use this 7 inch speaker and camera enabled "version" of Alexa. If you don't own one yet, then you may want to get one but of course go over every detail first so you can make a smart shopping choice.

Chapter 1: The Amazon Echo Show Out of the Box

It was June 28, 2017 when Amazon officially launched the Echo Show. It hit the virtual shelves of this giant online retailer and you can just imagine what the company's loyal customers were thinking.

How Much is It?

Well, if you're a fan of the Amazon Echo, Echo Dot, and Echo Spot then you might be game for a little upgrade. When the Echo Show was released its price was pegged at $229.99 – okay so rounding it off that is $230 to be honest.

Is the cost of getting one worth it? We'll let you answer that yourselves – the value of an object is subjective after all. However, 230 dollars compared to the $85 for an Amazon Echo is definitely a lot more money for anyone to pay.

Is there a discount for signing up for Amazon Prime, are there any discount offers? Amazon does have discount offers from time to time. For instance, you can get a 35% discount (about an $80 savings) if you buy it while it's part of Amazon's Choice list. You can also get a refurbished unit that will carry a 10% discount saving you about $20.

If a 200 dollar smart assistant with visuals is way too much for a one-time payment then you can opt to pay for it via a five month installment. That will cost you around $46 a month.

What Makes the Echo Show Different?

The big difference between this and the other Alexa devices is the obvious 7 inch screen. That screen is touch sensitive, which basically makes it work like a tablet. It also comes with a 5 megapixel front facing camera. And yes, it is also outfitted with a speaker just like other Echo devices – the speakers on this thing is a lot better than the original Echo version 1 – yes, the flagship model.

Camera eh? It's pretty decent camera (so, don't worry) and oh, did we mention that it is always on? Well, the next question is if the camera is on "always on" mode then does that mean it is watching you good citizens?

Well – yes, isn't that what always on means? Oh, since we're already on the "always on" issue about this smart speaker slash smart screen, you should also know that the microphone on this thing is also always on – but you should know that by now, right?

Well, it's the same basic issue anyway ever since Amazon released the very first Echo speaker. Of course it is listening – it's on standby waiting for you to say the wake word. The same is true for the Echo Show. The camera is always on and is also on standby mode.

If that gives you the creeps then here's something that might cool your nerves. It's a fact that there is no one in Amazon's HQ who is constantly monitoring your video streams. There are no surveillance screens and quite frankly no one from Amazon will be interested.

Are the microphone recordings or maybe video snippets stored in Amazon's hard drives? Of course not. Does that help calm your nerves? If not then you can always turn off the camera and the microphone. You can just use the manual button on the Echo Show to wake up Alexa and then you can issue a command.

What's in the Box?

When you get your Echo Show delivered, it's going to come in that same nice packaging that the other Alexa powered products always have. Shout out to Amazon for that. When you open the package you will see your device wrapped in plastic. There's also another plastic film or shield or whatever you call it on the touch screen.

It's a seven inch screen so it should fit nice and snug in your hand. Some people have complained about the Echo Show being too big or too wide but what you should really understand is that THIS IS NOT A TABLET. It's not going to replace your iPad.

It's a bit triangular-ish at the back and it will remain plugged into the wall socket – yes, some people complained that this product wasn't portable due to the wire or power cable. But again, this thing was designed not to fit in your pocket or for you to carry around wherever you go.

As a matter of fact the Amazon Echo Show was designed to stand on your counter or your table or whatever surface you might want to put it on. Now that we have that downside straightened out, let's go through with the rest of the stuff out of the box.

Just like with other Echo devices, you will also get a "Things to Try card" in the package – you know that little piece of paper with commands and other stuff that lets you try out the features of your Echo device. You will also get a little booklet with the instructions, which should tell you how to set the Show up.

Other than that you will also get the power cord slash plug. That one will go into the wall of course. Note that Amazon Echo Show will come in either of two colors – black or white. Pick the one that will match your interiors and décor. It's all up to you.

The Echo Show itself is very streamlined. There aren't that many buttons on it. You'll have three buttons at the top – one for mute and the other two buttons are for volume up and volume down. And that's pretty much it for manual controls and buttons.

You have a 7-inch touch screen but don't expect it to behave and function like a tablet. Out of the box you won't see much except for the home screen. You can change the wall paper through the Alexa app, that's one option. Another one is to have your Echo Show display different wall papers in a slide show.

The Echo Show also comes with two built in front facing speakers. Are those any better than the original Echo that Amazon launched way back when? The answer is yes. These speakers are much better if not louder than the ones installed on the original and they also carry more bass, which is great when you're listening to music.

Okay, that's it for the unboxing experience. In the next chapter we'll go over the setup process for the Echo Show.

Chapter 2: The Setup Process

The next thing you're going to do with a new Amazon Echo Show is to power it up, obviously. You plug the power cord at the back of the device and the other end you plug into the wall outlet. Note that there is no power button on the Show so once you plug it in it will power up automatically.

You will get to see a short video in the beginning telling you what the Echo Show can do. The visuals are good – is it the best for watching movies? Well, it's a 7 inch screen – we'll give you that but it's not the best movie watching experience, right?

However, the screen itself is pretty good and it's also very responsive. After watching the little snippet at initial startup everybody does pretty much the same thing – they go "uh, so... what's next?"

That's basically the initial experience you get when you setup your device. So, how do you setup your Echo Show? Check out the steps below:

What You Will Need

The entire setup process will take less than five minutes to complete – well, give or take a few. There are several factors involved. If there is a software update that needs to be downloaded then it will take a bit longer. If you have a spotty connection, then expect the update to take a bit longer than usual.

You should also have your WiFi network login details. Oh yes, you will also need your Amazon account credentials as well. Will you need your phone just in case? For this setup, nope, you won't need it. Everything else in the setup process will be done on the Show's display.

So, here's a rundown of everything you will need to setup your Echo Show:

- An Echo Show unit, of course
- An Amazon account – preferably an Amazon Prime account
- A router to run your WiFi connection
- An internet service
- Your smartphone, tablet, or computer (PC/Mac or Desktop/Laptop) anything that you can use to download an app.

Let's Get Started

Now, the first thing you need to have is the Alexa App. You will download that from the Amazon App Store. You can download it on your phone, laptop, desktop, or any other mobile device. The Alexa app supports the following operating systems:

- iOS 9.0 or higher
- Android 5.0 or higher
- FireOS 3.0 or higher

After downloading and installing the Alexa app you should find a good spot for your Amazon Echo Show. Now, it should be placed in a spot with good WiFi signal or else you won't get that good a performance from this device. Well, the same is true for any device that connects to your wireless network. It should also be at least 8 inches away from a wall or window if there is one close to it.

An alternative way to setup your Amazon Echo App is through your computer's browser. The following are the supported browsers for this setup:

- Internet Explorer (10 or higher)
- Microsoft Edge
- Chrome
- Safari
- Firefox

As stated earlier, there is no power button on the Amazon Echo Show. To start it up, all you need to do is to plug it to a wall outlet. It will boot up immediately as soon as you plug it in.

Once it is powered up – note that it powers up really quick unlike a computer – you will then hear Alexa say "Hello, your Echo Device is ready for setup." After that you will get an on screen prompt about the device's language setup. Select English (or whatever language you would like to use).

Logging Into Your Wireless Network

The next thing it will ask you to do after working on the language settings is to connect to a WiFi network – enter the login details necessary to connect to your wireless network. Note that there isn't any Ethernet port on the Echo Show so there's no way to plug it in directly to your router – that would have made everything much simpler though.

After that Alexa will ask you to confirm your time zone and then since it's already connected to the internet, it will ask you to login with your Amazon account details. Note that the account details you used to log into the Alexa app on your phone should be the same account that you will use to login this time.

You will then be asked to agree to the terms and conditions notice. If you're in luck then there should be no updates to install but since Alexa will check for any updates at this time then it may find one or two.

It's Time for Updates

If there is an update then you will get an update notification afterwards. The screen will display that updates for your device are ready. All you can do at this point is to tap on "Install Now."

The download and installation process will take a few minutes. Better get some coffee or any drink you can get. When the updates have been completely installed you will get a notification on the screen.

Introductory Video

Following the updates you will be shown the video called "Introducing Echo Show." Should you skip this video? We recommend that you take the time to watch it. Besides, it isn't that long and it will help you become familiar with the most common features and capabilities of your latest Echo device.

After watching the video Alexa will then tell you "Your Echo Show is ready." And that is pretty much all there is to it when it comes to setting up this device. In the next section of our guide we will go over a few tests that you can run.

That way you can check to see if there are any factory defects on your device. Well, everything should run smoothly if the setup process was successful. However, it doesn't hurt to test your Echo Show just to be sure, right?

Chapter 3: Tests and Initial Stuff You Can Do

Now, here are a bunch of fun and cool things you can try after a successful initial setup. You can say that this is your getting to know phase between you and the now visually enabled Alexa. If you already have an Echo device you can try the same commands here as well. However, note that some of the commands will be slightly different.

Now, sometimes Alexa will still have some trouble trying to understand what you are saying. There will be times when she will just freeze there after issuing a command. If it's your first time owning an Alexa powered smart assistant then you ought to know that your device is building a repository or profile of your voice.

In other words, it is recording a bunch of sound clips of your voice giving commands. The recordings will be stored online (i.e. cloud based storage). The longer time you spend with Alexa through your Amazon Echo Show (or some other Echo device) the better will she be able to understand your commands.

It's going to be hilarious sometimes when you give one command and Alexa does something else. It's either hilarious or it's going to be frustrating. The experience is going to be different each time. Give her time and Alexa will do better at listening to what you are saying.

The Colors on Your Home Screen

Now, before we move on to the commands and all the other fun stuff, let's go over the visuals you are getting from the home screen. Your home screen is the screen that you get when your Echo Show is all setup.

It's like your desktop screen on your computer and just like your phone it too has a wall paper, which you can change. We'll get to that in a minute. There are several visual indicators on your home screen that will give you a clue as to what Alexa is doing. The indicators are similar to the light indicators on the Echo, Echo Dot, and others.

- Blue colored indicator

You get a blue indicator status on your home screen when you use the wake word. The same wake words can be used for the Echo Show which includes Alexa, Amazon, Echo, and Computer. If you see a blue color on the home screen then it means your Echo Show is processing your request or command.

- Red colored indicator

If the color of your visual indicator is red then that means the microphone and the camera are turned off. To turn them on, press the on/off button at the top of the Amazon Echo Show. Now you know how to turn off the "always on" audio and video features of this device.

- Purple colored indicator

When you see a purple colored indicator on the home screen then this means your Echo Show is in *Do Not Disturb* mode. In this mode your Echo Show won't give you any alerts when someone calls or sends a message. It also blocks the "Drop In" function, which is pretty cool if you're looking for some private time. We'll go over the steps on how to turn the Do Not Disturb mode on and off and how to schedule one on your Echo Show in a later section of this guide.

- Orange color indicator

When the home screen is on orange then that means your Echo Show seems to be having trouble trying to connect to your wireless network. In case you can't get Alexa to do anything then one of the first things you need to check is the color of your home screen – if it's orange, now you know. We'll go over the connectivity troubleshooting for your Show in a later chapter.

Testing Your Echo Show's Voice Recognition

One of the things that we recommend that you do first is to test the voice recognition capability of your Echo Show. This is the way you can check if the microphone installed on your device is working properly.

Here are a few things you can try:

1. Wake word

Say the wake word. The default wake word is "Alexa." When you say the current wake word (you can change it later) the indicator color of the home screen will change to blue. Remember to say the wake word first every time you want to give a command or ask a question.

2. Funny stuff that you can ask

Now, we know that the voice that Amazon used for Alexa is kind of robotic. Well, they're working on it but as of the moment it doesn't compare to Tony Stark's Jarvis – that would have been so cool.

Well, however, here are a bunch of cool and funny things that you can ask or just tell Alexa so you can have a virtual conversation going on. Pay attention to how she responds to each of these things:

- I'm home!
- I love you.
- How are babies made?
- Why is water wet?
- Who's your favorite Pokemon?
- You're weird
- What do Lannisters do?
- What's the first rule of fight club?
- Do you have a sister?
- What's your zodiac sign?
- Do you do drugs?
- Do you get bored sometimes?
- What is a pie?
- What's your favorite food?
- Set the mood!
- What do we say to death?
- Beam me up.
- What are today's winning lottery numbers?
- Trick or treat!
- Say the alphabet.
- Launch crystal ball!
- Does every person on earth poop?

- Sing the auto tune.
- Are you Sky Net?
- Sing Twinkle Twinkle Little Star.
- Don't blink.
- How much is that doggie in the window?
- What is the first lesson of sword play?
- Why is the sky blue?
- Can you smell that?
- I'm going to bed.
- Are you alive?
- Did you pass the Turing test?
- Who is the real Slim Shady?
- What is the meaning of life?
- Where am I?
- Which came first, the chicken or the egg?
- What's the magic word?
- Who are you voting for?
- It's my birthday!
- What color are you?
- Meow!
- Testing 1, 2, 3.
- Sing the national anthem.
- Make me breakfast.
- Will pigs ever fly?
- Who's the boss?

We can't list all the questions that you can ask your Echo device. We'll the commands in the other sections of this book. Alexa can recognize a lot of questions and will give you either a verbal or visual response – or both. Sometimes when you ask your Echo device to do something, like scheduling something in a calendar or something then it will just do that task.

3. A Few Talk and Tap Tips

Now, you don't have to talk in a superficial voice when speaking to Alexa. Just talk in your normal voice or tone. Remember to speak at your normal pace. Remember that Alexa is trying to build a profile of the way you speak so she can interact better with you.

The touch screen on your Echo Show works just like your phone's screen. Apply the same amount of pressure when you press on it when scrolling or tapping – like you would on a regular tablet or even on an iPad.

To help you get more comfortable with your new Alexa powered device, try playing music. If you are subscribed to Amazon Prime Music then you can access your songs and playlists there via your Echo Show.

Try the following commands:

- Alexa, play [insert name of song and artist] from Prime Music.
- Alexa, play top 40 hits from Prime Music.
- Alexa, play rock from Prime Music.

Notice that when you play music, there will be lyrics displayed on the screen, which is great if you want to sing along – it's also a useful tool to check if you've been singing the right lyrics.

Now, when it comes to video back then you could stream YouTube videos through the Echo Show. However, somewhere along the way Amazon and Google had disputes so Google took away YouTube videos from the scene.

Now, even though you can no longer play YouTube videos on your Echo Show, you still have a pretty good selection of video options from Amazon Video. You still have Cinemax, Starz, Showtime, and HBO.

Try the following commands:

- "Alexa, show my watch list."
- "Alexa, show my video library"

Play around with your Echo Show for the mean time and try to discover some fun stuff you can do with it. We'll go over some settings and other features that you can work with in the next chapters.

Chapter 4: Saving WiFi Passwords to Amazon

Another thing that you should know about your Echo device is that whenever you go through the WiFi setup process, you have the option to save the password of your wireless network to Amazon. Yes, that means that password gets saved via Amazon's cloud service.

Is there any benefit when you do that? Well, it's a huge convenience in case you intend to connect multiple devices that you bought from Amazon. You won't have to reenter your WiFi password for each compatible device. The Alexa app will supply the passwords for you.

Now, imagine if you are running more than one wireless network. If you have one or a few devices switch from one network to the other then you won't have to bother entering the necessary credentials for every device that you own.

Security Concerns

Some people wonder if keeping their wireless network passwords will keep their network secure. Well, what we know for sure is that the passwords will be stored on Amazon's servers.

That means you are basically banking on the security features. Your password will be transmitted via a secure connection used by Amazon. And whatever encryption they use to store files on their servers will be the same level of protection your passwords get.

You won't have to worry about anyone sharing your wireless network login information to anyone.

Opting Not to Save Your Password

Is there a way to opt out of this service? Of course there is. You can do that when you connect your Amazon Echo Show (or any Echo device or other products from Amazon that also connects to WiFi).

Changing Wireless Network Password

You can change the wireless network password saved to Amazon by repeating the WiFi setup process for your Amazon Echo Show. When your Echo device is connected to the wireless network and regains internet access it will update the wireless network password stored in Amazon's servers.

Deleting Stored WiFi Passwords

Of course you can also delete any wireless network password that has been saved in Amazon's servers. You can do that by using a web browser. Here are the steps:

1. Login using your Amazon username and password.
2. On the Amazon website tap or click Manage Your Content and Devices
3. After that tap/click on Settings.
4. Go to Saved Wi-Fi Passwords
5. Click or tap Delete.

Chapter 5: Customizing Your Home Screen

The Home screen is a unique feature of the Alexa Echo Show simply because, well, it's the only product in its class that has one (at the moment at least). The home screen will usually display the time and weather, just like what your phone would have – except that there won't be icons there.

The home screen will also display command suggestions, which will help you communicate with Alexa a lot better – so pay attention to them. You will also find current events, events that you scheduled, and suggested voice commands displayed there from time to time.

Note that the home screen is customizable, which means you can change what can be displayed on it. You can choose what background photos your Echo Show should display and what cards will be displayed and other visual effects as well.

Navigating the Home Screen

Now, before you can customize your home screen, the first thing you should learn is how to navigate the Echo Show's touch screen itself. Don't worry; it's not as complicated as the navigation for your phone or tablet.

Here's how you navigate:

- **Home Screen** – If you have navigated to some area of the menu and you need to get back to the home screen in a flash just say "*Alexa, go home*" (of course you substitute/should use the wake word that you opted for). Another way to do it is by swiping downward from the top of the screen and then tapping on **Home**.
- **Check Settings** – Sometimes you may want to check the available settings for certain features. To do that you should swipe downward from the top of the screen on your Echo Show and then select **Settings**. Alternatively, you can say "Alexa, go to settings."
- **Scrolling** – Sometimes you will see a huge list of things on your screen, like the songs that you have purchased or maybe a list of recommended skills that are compatible with your Echo Show. You can scroll up and down through the list with your fingers as you would on a tablet or phone or you can say "Alexa, scroll up (or down, depending on which direction you would like the list to scroll to).

Setting Menu Options

To begin customizing your Amazon Echo Show's **Home** screen go to **Settings** using the steps described above. Within the Settings menu you will find a list of things you can modify. The list will include the following:

- **Bluetooth** – this is where you go to adjust Bluetooth settings.
- **Wi-Fi** – for wireless connectivity options.
- **Home Screen/Home & Clock** – this is for notifications, home cards, Drop In, upcoming events, and other reminders. We'll go over this in detail later.
- **Display** – this is where you go to adjust how your screen behaves like screen brightness, screen clock, photo slide shows, themes, and others.
- **Sounds** – this the section of the settings menu where you can adjust the Echo Show's volume, volume of the timers and notifications, media volume, and also the notification sounds you prefer to use.
- **Do Not Disturb** – this is where you setup your do not disturb mode. We'll talk about that in detail in a separate section of this guide.
- **Restrict Access** – this is where you restrict, modify, or block access to some of the settings and features of your Amazon Echo Show.
- **Device Options** – this is where you set remote pairing, time, location settings, and device name.
- **Things to try** – this is where you can find some of the cool things that Alexa suggests that you try.
- **Help** – need help with something about your Echo Show? This is where you can find them in a jiffy.
- **Accessibility** – This is where you can find accessibility options for your device. We'll go over these options in a later chapter.

- **Legal and Compliance** – this is where you'll find the terms and conditions of use for the Echo Show and also for Alexa as well.

Customizing Your Home Screen

Now that you know what's in the **Settings** list, it's time for you to go through **Home Screen** customization. In Settings, you should tap on Home Screen. You will then see two options – Background and Home Card Preferences.

Let us begin with your options for Background. Tap that and you will be given several options that you can customize. This will give you customization options for your home screen background. They include the following:

- **Default** – This is the first option right at the top. The default setting for your Echo Show is to use the images that are supplied from Amazon's photo library. That means you'd just let Echo Show choose from the images that the manufacturer has supplied. Well, some of them are great but you can't really say that they will do wonders for your décor. This will also be the default setting that the Echo Show will be on – i.e. it will already be selected. If you don't like the default photos that came straight out of the factory or maybe you've gotten tired of seeing them day in and day out – don't worry. The good news is that there are still other options for the screen background.

- **Alexa App Photo** – If you don't like the current background photos used by your Echo Show, you can change them yourself by uploading a photo to your device via the Alexa App.

    So, how do you do that? Here are steps:
1. Tap on *Alexa App Photo*
2. Your Echo Show will then prompt you that you should use your Alexa App to upload a photo. Now, open your phone, tablet, or computer that has the app installed on it and login with your Amazon credentials.

3. On the Alexa App, you should tap or click the menu button. And then after that go to Settings (it's usually at the bottom and it's the one with the cog wheel to its left).
4. You'll see a list of Alexa devices there. Select your Echo Show from the list (note that some people rename their Echo Show on the Alexa App via the Show's settings as described in the Settings options above).
5. And then you will see a huge blue colored "CHOOSE A PHOTO" button. It's just below the **Home Screen Background** menu option.
6. That will pull up a file picker and it will display all the available photos that you can choose from. Tap the photo you would like to use as the background photo or picture of your Amazon Echo Show.
7. You can zoom in, crop, or adjust the area of the photo you selected that should be displayed on your Echo Show screen.
8. Now, tap the blue UPLOAD button on the bottom right of the screen and then your Alexa App will upload the edited version of the photo to your Echo Show.

- **Home Card Preferences** – This is the second option on the list. There are several options under this menu. Note that home cards include the items displayed on your Echo Show's home screen like the weather, news, events, and others.

They include the following:

1. **Rotation** – This allows you to choose how often your Echo Show will rotate the home cards (i.e. switch from one card to the next). You will see two options when you tap on this home card preference – Rotate Once and Rotate Continuously.

> The default setting is Rotate Continuously. That means your Echo Show will cycle from one home card to the next repetitively. Rotate once on the other hand means that your Echo Show will just display all the cards on the home screen one after the other once whenever you display the home screen. If you want to see the other home screen cards you will have to swipe left or right to view them.

2. **Toggles** – You'll find these under the Rotation options. There are four items that you can toggle on or off – (1) Notifications, (2) Upcoming Events, (3) Drop In, and (4) Trending Topics – you might have to scroll down a little bit to toggle this last option on or off.

> Notifications – you switch this on or off if you want your Echo Show to display alerts about voice commands you can try, new skills that have been launched for your device, and others. Upcoming Events on the other hand will display some sort of reminder about events that you scheduled on your calendar.

> If you toggle Drop In to On then your Amazon Echo Show will display which of your contacts are online and call using this feature. The last item you can toggle is Trending Topics, which basically is a home card that shows you the news headlines. You toggle which of

these items you want to display or not on your Echo Show home screen. It's all up to you.

That's pretty much how you can customize your home screen to your liking. Some features have their upsides and downsides – like when you upload a photo through the Amazon App, sure you can customize the background picture but it doesn't do a slide show, which some people would like. The good news is that you can make these changes really fast and without much hassle.

Chapter 6: Connecting Bluetooth Speakers

So far we know that the Echo Show has better speakers compared to the original Amazon Echo. It has a richer and much fuller sound plus a nice bass to it as well. That should come as no surprise since it should be the next upgrade in this product series.

However, good as they can be, you shouldn't compare these built in speakers to your surround sound system. It's obviously no match for it no matter how you look at it.

The good news is that the Alexa Echo Show is Bluetooth enabled. That means you can connect other speakers (obviously the much better sounding ones that you have in the house) and get a better vibe at home.

A Few Preliminaries

Now, before we go over the steps on how to connect third party speakers via Bluetooth, let's go over a few setup preliminaries – well, you know, just to make sure that everything goes fine. Now, here are a few things you have to remember:

- Your Echo Show should be at least three feet away from the Bluetooth speaker(s) you intend to use. Doing this helps with connectivity and to avoid feedback.
- The Bluetooth speaker you should pair with your Echo Show should be certified. That means it is compatible with Echo devices. In a later section of this chapter, we'll go over the Bluetooth profiles that are supported by your Echo Show.

- To check if your Bluetooth speaker is functioning properly, you should try to connect it to other devices that are also Bluetooth enabled such as your phone.
- When you're going through the setup process, remember to turn on your Bluetooth speaker and also to turn up the volume.
- You should also remember that your Amazon Echo Show can only connect to only one Bluetooth enabled device at a time. Some people forget that their Echo Show is already connected to another Bluetooth device when they connect a wireless speaker. Make sure that the other Bluetooth devices are disconnected and then connect your speaker.

Connecting a Bluetooth Speaker

Here are the steps you need to do in order to connect a Bluetooth speaker:

1. The first thing you need to do is to turn on your Bluetooth speaker's pairing mode. Each speaker will require different steps on how to do this so please just refer to the instructions that came with your speaker.

2. Go to Settings on your Amazon Echo Show either by swiping from the top going downwards and then tapping Settings or just say "Alexa, go to settings."

3. Within your Show's settings select Bluetooth.

4. After that, your Echo Show will enter its pairing mode. It will then scan for available devices.

5. It will discover your Bluetooth speakers and it will get listed on the screen as one of the available Bluetooth devices. If you have other Bluetooth devices that are already enabled then you will also see them on this list.

6. Select your Bluetooth speakers from the list and follow the rest of the on screen prompts.

7. Alexa will then inform you that the connection was successful.

Okay, so what if you want to turn things around – what if you want to stream music to your Echo Show from a Bluetooth enabled device like say your phone? Here's how you can do that:

1. Turn your Alexa Echo Show's Bluetooth on by saying "Alexa, pair my phone."

2. Open the Bluetooth on your phone and then select your Echo Show in the list of Bluetooth devices.

3. Alexa will then tell you that the connection was successful.

4. Start streaming your music from your phone.

Playing Multi-Room Music

You can take your music experience to the next level by playing them all throughout the house. This works if you have multiple Echo devices in the house. That way when you play your music you can have it playing through different speakers and sound systems.

If you have an Echo in living room, an echo dot in the other rooms, and maybe an Echo Show in the kitchen, then you can have them play the same music simultaneously. So, how do you set that up? In a nutshell, here's how you can do it:

1. Open the Alexa app
2. Select **Smart Home** from the menu items.
3. Select **Create Groups**, which will create a device group
4. Select **Multi-Room Music Group**

5. At this point you can either create a custom music group by tapping on **Create Custom** or choose a preexisting group that is already on the list.
6. Tap on **Next**
7. Alexa will then confirm the group that you have selected or created
8. Now, ask Alexa to play a song, album, songs from a particular artist or whatever you have going there and then mention the group name that you created/selected.
9. Now you will hear the same music played across different Alexa powered devices.

Chapter 7: Viewing and Displaying Photos

Here's a neat trick that you can do with your Amazon Echo Show – turn it into a digital photo frame. Well, since the Echo Spot also has a screen then of course the tips and tricks mentioned here will work for that as well. That is if you also have an Echo Spot.

What's a digital picture frame? It's basically like any regular picture frame only that you don't have a printed photo in there. You can use your own photos as a background image and you can also use them as a wall paper for your screen.

Which Photos Do I Use?

Your Echo Show will allow you to use multiple photos for your background image or you can just opt to use one – again, it's all up to you. Here's an idea, use multiple photos as background images and just use your favorite pic as the wallpaper.

As stated earlier, when you have multiple photos available for your use you can have your Echo Show display them in slide show fashion. Note that while you're at it, your Echo Show might even suggest photos for your background image (or images) depending on a certain theme.

Alexa can suggest which pictures to use from your digital photo library and can pick photos out depending on certain categories such as recent photos, locations, mountains, or beach for instance.

Now, let's say you have lots of photos of the beach. You can sort of make it a theme for your digital photo frame and have it display only photos of you on the beach. Now, here's a neat trick – setup a Family Photo Vault (a feature available for Amazon Prime Members) you can use photos uploaded by your family and then use them as your Echo Show's background image or wallpaper.

So, how do you setup a **Family Photo Vault**?

1. If you already have an Amazon Prime Account then point your browser to Amazon Prime Photos (*https://www.amazon.com/b/?node=13234696011*)
2. Click on the orange **Get Started** button that is slightly to the right of the screen.
3. You will then be asked to log in to your Amazon Prime account.
4. After that you can start sending invites so you can add more people to your group. Note that invites are sent via email. You only have the option to add up to 5 people in your family group. In the Invite People to Your Family Vault window, click the Send Invitation button.
5. After that, you can start adding photos (i.e. from the ones that you have uploaded to the Prime Photos page) to your new Family Photo Vault.
6. You can use the filters on the left side of the page or just view them as they are arranged by upload date by default.
7. Put a check on the photos you want to add to your Family Vault and then click on **Add to Family Vault** which you can find at the top of the page. Another option is to just click **Add All**. It makes sense, well since Amazon offers unlimited storage for your photos. Note that the Family Vault also includes a 5 gigabyte storage space for videos you might want to upload as well.

Displaying Photos on Your Amazon Echo Show

There are two ways that you can use to display your photos on the Echo Show as a background pic. You can do that either through the settings on your Echo Show or through the Alexa app on your phone.

Here's how you do that on the Alexa app:

1. Launch your Alexa app
2. Tap on **Settings** from the menu on the side.
3. Select your Amazon Echo Show.
4. Next, you need to scroll down until you find **Home & Clock Background**
5. Tap on the blue CHOOSE A PHOTO button.
6. Tap on the photo that you want to use as your background.

Of course you can also do that on the Echo Show itself. The cool thing here is that if you have Prime Photos you can use a series of photos to make a background slide show as stated above.

We already covered how to setup Prime Photos and the Family Photo Vault service from Amazon. In order to access those photos and use them as background images for your Echo Show you need to install the Prime Photos app.

You can download the app for the Fire Tablet here:

https://www.amazon.com/Amazon-com-Prime-Photos-from-Amazon/dp/B00A11AN6O

You can download the app for the iPhone and iPad here:

https://itunes.apple.com/us/app/prime-photos-from-amazon/id621574163?mt=8

You can download the app for Android devices here:

https://www.dropbox.com/s/bso6fxxh1pufq2n/Screenshot%202018-04-17%2013.47.27.png?dl=0

Here's how you setup your photos as background images using your Echo Show:

1. Swipe downward from the top of the screen and then select **Settings**.
2. Go to Home Screen
3. Next, you need to select Background
4. After that select Prime Photos
5. And then tap on Change.

You will be shown pictures and albums that you can use as the background image. Note that Alexa will also make suggestions, which sort of makes things easier. Note that if you choose more than one photo for your background they will be displayed in slide show fashion.

You can use your recent photos if you like. You can also display a slide show of pictures according to location. Note that the pictures that you select will cycle every ten minutes.

If you just want to view your photos on the Echo Show in a **slide show**, then do the following using the touch screen:

1. Swipe down from the top
2. Tap on Settings
3. Tap on Display
4. Select the item **Photo Slideshow**
5. Tap **Slideshow Speed** and then select the speed you want for your slideshow.

NOTE: There is a camera on your Echo Show and it can be used to take photos and other snapshots. In the next chapter we'll talk about how to use this camera to make video calls. The pictures that you take using the Show's camera will automatically be uploaded to your library of Prime Photos.

Here's how you take photos using the camera that you can use as a background later on:

- Say "Alexa, take a photo" – your Echo Show takes a single snapshot. You can also add stickers to your pic. Just swipe on your picture and you'll see the available stickers that you can use.
- Say "Alexa, take a Four Shot photo." Your Echo Show will then four pictures in a sequence that have been cropped into one single photo.

Using Voice Commands to Set Up Your Background

Now, if you think that going through all those menu items and navigating a setup screen is just way too tedious then you can use voice commands to set up your Echo Show's background screen.

Now, just as the way it was done on the Echo Show screen, you should already have photos ready and uploaded via your Prime Photos app so that Alexa can set things up for you.

Here's how you setup your background using voice commands:

1. Say "Alexa, show my photos" and then your photos will be displayed on the Amazon Echo Show.
2. Alternatively, if you have your albums already saved, then you can tell Alexa to display the pictures from specific albums. To do that, say "Alexa, show my" and then mention the name of the album. Remember to use the current wake word you selected, which means you don't necessarily have to use "Alexa."

Note that when you tell Alexa to show you your pictures from a certain album, then she will slide show each photo really fast. If you want, you can always pause, resume slide show, move to the next pic, or see the previous pic via voice commands.

Use the following commands – note that while Alexa is showing you a slide show of your photos you don't have to say the wake word when using these commands:

- Previous
- Next
- Pause
- Resume

Use the following command to set your background:

"Alexa, set this as my background"

Or

"Alexa, set this album as my background"

Alexa will then tell you that she is setting your selected album as your background. But if you want to set a single photo sa your background use the following command:

"Alexa, set this photo as my background"

Chapter 8: Phone and Video Calls

In the world of smartphones, sometimes it doesn't make sense to have a phone that's stuck to the wall, right? Like come on – what if you were on the move? Having a phone that is absolutely mobile is the way to go right?

That may be true in a lot of situations but there are times when you need to answer a phone call or make a phone call when both of your hands are full. How do you answer a phone call like that?

So there are times when a fixed phone that you can activate by voice command and one that is stuck to the wall to boot does make sense. In fact it can even be the obvious choice. Imagine being in the kitchen and you're making delicate pastry work and you just realized that you needed to call somebody.

Your hands are dirty and you don't have the time to wash them, make that call, and then wash them all over again because you need to get back to kneading and dusting your dough. Another downside of a mobile phone is the fact that it runs on batteries – if its batteries run out then you have no choice but to charge it. You don't get that with a stationary phone.

With the help of your Amazon Echo Show you don't have to miss a single call again. Even if you have your phone plugged in to the wall and charging while you're in the other room, you can still answer that phone call via your Echo Show (or some other Echo device as well since this is an Alexa feature).

Other than improving your chances to answer important phone calls, your Echo Show also makes it easy to make quick calls to other people especially if you were also in the middle of something.

Connect Your Phone to Your Amazon Echo Show

In order to connect your Echo Show to your phone, you need to use the Alexa App. Remember that when you installed it you were requested to confirm your phone number. You entered your phone number plus the six digit Amazon code that you needed to enter which the Amazon system sent to your number via text. This code is used to verify that the phone number you entered is really yours.

Now, there are phones that have two factor authentication. You just need to enter your email address and verify that too. You will go through pretty much the same process as the one earlier that involved SMS authentication.

Open the Alexa app and then tap the chat bubble that you will find at the bottom of the screen – it's the icon in the middle at the bottom to be exact. After that, tap the person icon that you will find at the very top of the screen. It's on the upper right hand corner.

That will bring up a list of contacts. These contacts were derived from your list of contacts that is currently stored in your phone. There is a downside to making Alexa to Alexa calling – this is a bit of an FYI so as to set the proper expectations. In order for this to work your contacts must also have the Alexa app installed on too.

Well, you don't have to coerce your friends, family, and coworkers to buy their own Amazon Echo Show – though that would be cool too. But you can at least ask them to install the Alexa app on their phones so that you can answer or call them through your Echo Show or another Alexa device.

However, it should come as a relief that your Echo Show can still make calls even if the receiving party doesn't have an Alexa powered device or even the Alexa app installed. It will be just like a regular phone call without the extra features – we'll get to those extras in a minute.

Now, to make a call (or an Alexa to Alexa call), tap the person's name or alternatively you can give the following command:

"Alexa, call [insert contact's name]"

If you have setup multiple phone numbers on your list of contacts then you can specify which of that contact person's number to call. Here's an example of that:

"Alexa, call Bob's mobile number"

Or

"Alexa, call Jerry's work number."

Okay so you get the drill. Now, here are the extras. In case the person you are calling also has a compatible Echo device then you will see a video call icon on your Alexa app. You will also see the light indicator bar on your Echo Show turn green.

If you have other Alexa powered devices you will notice that their light rings will also turn green. To answer the call, give the following command to Alexa:

"Answer"

Alternatively you will also see a green answer button on your Echo Show's screen. Tap that and you answer the call. On the other hand, you can tap the red "end" button and you drop the call or don't answer the call. Alternatively you tell Alexa "Ignore" if you don't want to answer the call.

Note that Alexa will tell you who is calling, which is something good to know in certain circumstances. Your Echo Show will also display the name of the contact who is calling.

On the Alexa app, you may see a video call button in the middle of your contact list. Tap this button to start a video call *after* answering the call. So, how do you initiate a video call on your Amazon Echo Show? To do that, use the following command:

"Video on"

If you want to turn video calling off, just say:

"Video off"

You have a couple of options in case you want to end a call using your Echo Show. The first one is by tapping the screen. You will see two buttons on the screen. Tap the yellow or red "end" button (it's the one on the lower left corner of the screen). Note that the other button is the video call button. Alternatively you can just tell Alexa to:

"Hang up"

And that will end the call.

Chapter 9: Drop In Feature and Do Not Disturb Mode

One of the innovative things that Amazon has done since they launched their line of Alexa enabled products is the ability of one Echo device to call and message one another. Back then you can use one smart speaker and call a friend who has one too.

With the addition of a built in camera and screen, the experience is taken up a notch with the Amazon Echo Show. Now you can video call or video chat with someone from across the room inside the house (or some other part of the house) to anyone across the globe.

New Features for New Alexa Devices

Well, video chat or video messaging isn't a new thing since you can already do that with your phone or tablet. Being able to do that on a fixed screen that you don't have to hold in your hands, well, that's like using an intercom. That means if you're video calling with someone across the globe then it's a worldwide intercom. Well, not exactly.

Apart from that Amazon introduces a few new features. One of those new features is the Drop In feature. It has its pros and cons but it can be quite useful. **Drop In** allows you to check in on someone through the Echo Show and they don't really need to answer. It's like virtually dropping in on someone unannounced (I think that's what they should have called this thing right from the start).

If you prefer more privacy, seriously who doesn't, this feature can be annoying to you. Imagine if you're really busy – say rushing to prepare food for guests – and then someone drops in on your Echo Show and they see what you're doing and they start talking to you and the really annoying thing is that it's not like a phone call.

You can't ignore and don't answer the call. With the Drop In feature the call proceeds whether you want to or not. Well, you can imagine how useful this could be if you are a parent especially if you're away from home and your kids are home alone – or are they?

You can **Drop In** and see exactly what they're doing when you're away. Well, now you're using your Echo Show like a video monitor. The big difference is that you can talk to your kids (or anyone in the house for that matter) and not just take a sneak peek. Yep, it's more interactive than you think.

That's actually not all the features that Amazon rolled out for their Alexa powered devices. They also released an intercom function, which can also be pretty useful. This feature allows you to broadcast a short voice message to a specific Alexa device.

Another feature that was also rolled out is Announcements. It's pretty much like an intercom function but it broadcasts your voice message to a group of Alexa devices instead of just one. It's a great way to tell everyone in the house that dinner is ready. Now you don't have to shout to call everybody in. We'll go over these features in this chapter.

Drop In

As stated earlier, the Drop In feature is not exactly like a regular phone call or video call. If one of your contacts decided to drop in on you then you have no option but to receive it. However, the good news is that you have few seconds to fix your hair or at least get out of the sight of the Echo Show's camera. The video feed will be slightly blurred for a few seconds and then it will clear up – should be enough to fix your lipstick or something.

Drop In connects automatically. That means you can talk to whoever is dropping in on you. That also means you can immediately hear the person on the other end of the line. Yes, it works both ways so both you (i.e. the one receiving the call) and the caller get the same experience. Of course the one dropping in will have that slight advantage – obviously.

Note that the Drop In feature is not exclusive to your Echo Show. Any device that has Alexa on it can Drop In on other Alexa users, but there are provisions of course. Now, here's a little catch that you should know about – you can initiate a Drop In using your smartphone that has the Alexa app installed but it can't receive a Drop In on your phone – i.e. only Alexa devices can receive a Drop In.

Simply put, if you want to use the Drop In feature you at least need one phone with the Alexa app installed and an Echo device, such as your Amazon Echo Show. The phone obviously will be the one to initiate the Drop In. Now, even though your phone can't receive a Drop In from your phone you can at least receive voice calls from your Echo Show or some other Alexa enabled device.

Setting Up Drop In

1. Note that you need to sign up for the Calling and Messaging service from Amazon.
2. Next, you need to open your Alexa app on your phone and then tap the chat bubble or conversations icon (it's the one at the bottom of the screen).
3. You may need to enter your name and your phone number especially if you are setting this up for the first time. Follow other on screen prompts as necessary.
4. Note that you should see that Drop In is enabled – it is enabled by default, which can be a bit annoying for some people.
5. Now here's another tedious step, you must check if it is on for each Alexa device you own. To do that go to Settings and then select your Echo Show (or another Alexa enabled device like the Echo Spot). In the page for that device check under **General** and go to **Drop In**. Select **On** in the options (well, it should be set to On in the first place but change it if it isn't).
6. If you want to use the **Drop In** feature only within your family then under the **Drop In** setting select **Only My Household**.

Allowing Drop In on Your Amazon Echo Show

Now, here's a good thing that Amazon did – they set things up so that no one can just Drop In to contact you by default. Well, a lot of serious privacy concerns were raised and of course a lot of people felt that it is a really intrusive feature. Thank you Amazon!

Nowadays, you will have to enable certain contacts or more specifically you should allow them to use the Drop In feature so that they can contact you. The same way is true if you want to use Drop In on your contacts. In short, they must also enable this feature first and set permissions so that you can contact them through this feature.

Best practice is that you should only allow this feature on contacts that you trust or for really close friends and family. So, how do you enable Drop In for a contact? Here are the steps:

1. Launch your Alexa app on your phone
2. Open the **Conversations** tab.
3. There is a contact icon that you will see on the top right of the screen – yes it's the one that looks like a person. Tap that icon.
4. You will then see a list of contacts that you can scroll through.
5. Select the contact that you want to enable for the Drop In feature.
6. Go to **Contact can Drop In Anytime** and toggle it so as to enable Drop In.

So, what if you want to disable this feature for one or a few contacts? Let's say you get annoyed by them and you no longer want them the privilege of dropping in on you. Here's what you can do to get that done:

1. Open your Alexa app on your smartphone
2. Select yourself on the list
3. Go to Others **Who Can Drop In on My Devices**.

4. You will see a list of contacts who are allowed to use Drop In to contact you.
5. Select a contact and then tap **Remove**. This will remove them from the contacts that you have allowed to use the Drop In feature on your Echo devices.

What if you want to disable Drop In only temporarily? The way to do that is to enable the Do Not Disturb mode on your Amazon Echo Show. We'll go over that later in the next chapter.

How to Drop In on your Contacts?

Using the Drop In feature to contact someone is really easy. Use the following command:

"Alexa, drop in on [say the contact's name]"

That's basically how you do it on your Amazon Echo Show. You can also manually initiate a Drop In using the Alexa app on your smartphone or iPhone. Here's how you can do that on your phone:

1. Open your Alexa app.
2. Open the conversations tab
3. Select a someone you want to contact using the Drop In feature.
4. Note that this should be a contact that has allowed you to use Drop In on them.
5. If that is correct then select Drop In, which you can see at the top in the blue bar.
6. Alternatively tap your Contacts button (the one on the right side).
7. Choose a contact in the list
8. Tap the Drop In icon located under the contacts name
9. Drop In will then connect with your selected contact and you will see them on your screen.

Note that the video feed on your screen (phone or Echo Show or what not) will be blurred out for a few seconds. It will then get cleared out after a few seconds.

Echo to Echo Drop In

So, how do you Drop In on your own Alexa devices? Let's say you have an Amazon Echo in the living room and you have an Echo Show in the kitchen. Here's how you can Drop In on your Echo Show so you can see and talk to anyone in the kitchen:

1. Say, "Alexa, show my contacts"
2. After then tap on your own contact card on your Echo Show
3. Tap the Drop In icon on your Show's screen.
4. After that you will see a list of Echo devices that you have registered.
5. Tap on the device and then initiate Drop In.

Alternatively you can say "Alexa, Drop In on [mention the name of your selected Echo device]"

Of course, if you have more than one Echo Show and you have other Alexa devices it makes sense to assign different names to them. Here's how you edit the names of each your Alexa enabled devices in the house:

1. Open your Alexa app
2. Open the menu on the upper left corner of the screen
3. After that tap on Alexa devices
4. Select a device in the list
5. You will find the name of your device under the General section
6. Tap on Edit Name
7. Enter the new name and save it.

How to End Drop In Call

To end a Drop In call all you need to say is "Alexa, hang up" and Alexa will end the call for you. Alternatively you can tap the Echo Show screen and then tap the red "End" button at the bottom.

Note that you can always turn off the video on your Amazon Echo Show any time. That is a big relief in case you're not ready for an actual video call; so you can just have a voice conversation. To turn off the video say "Alexa, video off."

That's a bit of convenience – someone drops in and you can immediately turn off the video, put on the right shirt or fix your make up and then turn the video on again. To turn the video back on say "Alexa, video on" or just say "video on."

Using Your Echo Show as a Household Intercom

Step 1

Now, before you can use Alexa devices as a kind of intercom in the home you should first give each one of them a separate name. Follow the instructions above to change the name of each of your Echo devices.

A good idea would be to give each device a room name depending on which room you placed it. You can have an Echo Show in the kid's room, you can have another Echo Show in the kitchen, an Echo dot in the bedroom will be a great idea – i.e. it's the less intrusive option, an original Amazon Echo in the living room, and maybe other Echo devices in the other rooms.

Step 2

After editing their names of each of your Echo devices, the next step is to enable Drop In for all your Echo devices so that you can use that feature to contact any Alexa enabled device you have in your home. Again, follow the instructions on how to do that mentioned above.

Step 3

Use Drop In to contact any of your Echo devices in the home. To do that say "Alexa, Drop In on [say the Echo device's name]." Here's an example:

"Alexa, call my Living Room Echo Show."

Remember to substitute the wake word that you specified.

Using the Announcements Feature

Now, here's a neat trick – do you want to have your actual voice broadcast through your Echo devices? It will be a fun trick to do at home especially if your kids aren't paying attention or something. You can call it your full in ghost mode!

To do that, say:

"Alexa, tell everyone [insert your message here]"

Or you can also say:

"Alexa, broadcast [insert your message here]"

Now, this will broadcast your message to all the Echo devices in the house. Here are a few sample messages that you can try on your Echo Show:

- Alexa, tell everyone that it's time to sleep.
- Alexa, tell announce that it's time to leave.
- Alexa, tell everyone that dinner is ready.

Note that you can also make announcements through the Alexa app on your mobile device. Now, here's another neat trick – you will hear sound effects along with your announcements.

To do that, use the following voice commands:

1. "Alexa, tell everyone it's time to wake up" or "Alexa, tell everyone rise and shine" – you will hear a rooster crow.
2. "Alexa, tell everyone love you" – you will hear the sound effect for playful kiss
3. "Alexa, tell everyone that breakfast is ready" – Alexa rings a dinner bell.
4. "Alexa, tell everyone that it's time to eat," – Alexa also rings a dinner bell.

5. "Alexa, tell everyone let's watch TV" or "Alexa, tell everyone that the movie is about to start" – Alexa will play show tune sound effect.
6. "Alexa, tell everyone congratulations!" or "Alexa, tell everyone way to go!" – Alexa will play a cheering sound effect.
7. "Alexa, say goodnight everyone" or "Alexa, tell everyone sleep tight" – you will hear a yawning sound effect.

Of course, this will be a useful feature to gather the entire family. Let's say you're already too tired because you slaved in the kitchen to make that special dinner. Who's got time to run around the house to announce that you're done cooking and the table is ready for eating.

Of course, the sound effects can become annoying. However, the guys from Amazon are still working on them so expect more effects to along and maybe more fine-tuned options as well. Remember that Alexa is continually growing so expect to see more and better options.

Enabling the Do Not Disturb Mode

Okay so not everyone is delighted with the Drop In feature. Technically speaking Drop In is an opt-in feature – it's something that you have to agree to. As illustrated above, you have to approve a contact before they can use this feature to contact you.

However, the thing that frustrates a lot of users is that this feature is enabled by default. Well, it is annoying and it is strange given the fact that Amazon already puts it as an opt-in. It isn't even a main feature. And that is why the **Do Not Disturb Mode** comes like a blessing in disguise.

So, what is the **Do Not Disturb Mode**?

When the Do Not Disturb Mode is turned on your Echo Show won't give out any alerts and notifications. That means you won't get any messages and calls. On top of that you also won't get any Drop In calls.

You can enable and disable this mode either by voice command or through the Alexa app. You can also schedule certain Do Not Disturb days or times.

Here are the voice commands that you can use to enable the Do Not Disturb Mode:

- Alexa, don't disturb me
- Alexa, turn on do not disturb.

If you want to turn off Do Not Disturb Mode, then say the following:

- Alexa, turn off Do Not Disturb.

Here's how you can use the Alexa App to turn on the Do Not Disturb Mode:

1. Launch the Alexa app on your phone.

2. Tap on the Menu icon – it's those three short horizontal lines at the top left corner of your screen.
3. Tap Settings – it's the one with the cog wheel at the bottom of the menu to the left.
4. You will see a list of Echo devices that you have enabled.
5. Select the Echo device from the list – let's say your Echo Show.
6. In the next window toggle the setting for Do Not Disturb to on so that it will get enabled.
7. You will also notice that the setting below that (i.e. Scheduled) is disabled by default.
8. If you want to schedule a Do Not Disturb Mode then tap Scheduled below and then switch it to **On**.
9. Enter the times and schedules when you want the Do Not Disturb mode to be enabled.
10. Tap the blue Edit button.

Chapter 10: Accessibility Features

A Little History about Accessibility

Accessibility is a big thing for Alexa, the smart assistant behind the Amazon's Echo products. As a bit of an FYI, the voice used for Alexa and of course Alexa herself has a bit of history when it comes to accessibility.

You see, many years ago, before Alexa was called Alexa she used to be called by a different name – Amy. Amy (the original version of Amazon's Alexa today) is the creation of Ivona Software.

Ivona Software is a Poland based company that produces accessibility products for disabled persons. At one point Ivona was commissioned by the Royal National Institute of Blind People to build voices using their trademarked speech to text technology.

The voices were designed to aid blind folks to read magazines and newspapers. One of the voices that were designed for blind listeners back then was Amy – the female voice that the company built. And in 2013 Ivona Software as acquired by Amazon and their Amy voice was developed into Alexa today.

Those in the UK who have used Amy as their voice and accessibility assistant recognized Alexa when when the original Echo was rolled out. Of course Amazon only wanted to create a product that can be pretty useful and one would sell very well to a lot of their customers.

Well, that was the original intent. However, little did Jeff Bezos and the think tank in Amazon realized that Alexa will later prove to be a godsend to a lot of handicapped folks not only in the UK but around the globe as well.

Alexa's Accessibility Features

There are several accessibility features that are built into the Amazon Echo Show and other Alexa enabled devices. These features include color correction, color inversion, screen magnification, and also closed captioning. Another useful feature that is well worth mentioning is VoiceView.

It is actually a screen reader that reads your gestures, which is used to tell Alexa how to navigate your Echo Show's screen. It is also that feature that gives you a spoken feedback about the screen items that a user picks as the menu is navigated.

Note that all of these features are designed to help customers who are vision or hearing impaired. Note that your Amazon Echo Show will behave and function a bit differently whenever the accessibility features are turned on.

For example, in case your Echo Show's touch screen is not responding every time you touch it, swipe, or maybe tap on an item you may have accidentally activated an accessibility feature, like the built in screen reader called VoiceView.

The news is that you can toggle VoiceView on and off just like any other feature on your Echo Show. Here are a few options that you can try to switch this feature on or off:

- Press and hold the mute button (i.e. the mic and camera button – the left most button at the top). After that your Echo Show will sound an alert. When that happens place two of your fingers on the screen (usually the index and middle finger – make sure that these two fingers will touch the screen slightly apart).

  Remember to touch the screen and hold it on for five seconds. Then that will automatically turn the accessibility features off. Repeat the same process if you want to enable them on your Echo Show.

- If the touch screen works and you aren't getting any response from your Echo Show and you suspect that its accessibility features are on, then check out the settings and toggle them on or off. To do that, swipe downward from the top of the screen and go to Settings > Accessibility > VoiceView Screen Reader > VoiceView.

NOTE: remember when you went through the initial setup process, VoiceView was one of the few prompts that flashed on your screen. You were given the option to set it up or not. Most likel you just skipped that part of the process.

Vision Settings on Your Echo Show

The following are some of the vision settings that you can toggle on or off:

- *VoiceView Screen Reader:* you toggle this feature on or off. It also has options like reading volume, adjusting the reading speed, gestures, and others.
- *Screen Magnifier:* here you adjust the settings on how your gestures can adjust the screen magnification.
- *Color Inversion:* this is the section where you can invert the screen colors. If it is easier to read text in white color then you can do just that here.
- *Color Correction:* this part is very useful for people who are color blind. You adjust color correction settings depending on the type of color blindness you may be experiencing which includes the following: Tritanomaly (blue-yellow), Protanomaly (red-green), and Deuteranomaly (red-green).

Hearing Settings on the Echo Show

The following are hearing settings that you can toggle on or off:

- *Closed Captioning:* this is where you adjust your captions for movie trailers and other videos. Tap on Closed Captioning Preferences to adjust the settings that control the appearance of the captions.
- *Alexa Captioning:* If you want to see closed captions of Alexa's responses on your screen then this is where you toggle it on. Select Alexa Captioning Preferences to customize the captions.
- *Calling and Messaging without Speech:* this is Alexa's messaging touch feature that allows you to see transcripts of messages you had with your contacts.

How to Use Alexa and Closed Captioning on the Amazon Echo Show

Some movies and videos are easier to understand with subtitles and closed captions. To enable this feature on your Echo Show, follow the steps below:

1. Swipe downward from the top of your Echo Show's screen and then select Settings. Alternatively you can tell Alexa to "Go to settings."
2. Within Settings tap on Accessibility
3. Toggle Closed Captioning to **On** or **Off** to enable or disable this feature.

To see Alexa's responses in your interaction with her, turn on Alexa Captioning. Here's how you do that:

1. Tell Alexa to "Go to settings," or you can swipe downward from the top of the screen and then select **Settings**.
2. From Settings, tap on Accessibility.

3. Go to Alexa Captioning and toggle it to On or Off.

Remember that not all of Alexa's responses will be captioned even if you enable Alexa Captioning. Note that when you change the style settings for Closed Captioning, it doesn't change the style settings for other captioning features. You need to set style preferences separately. On top of that, only Closed Captioning text will be seen when you watch videos and movies.

The following are the captioning preferences that you can toggle on or off:

- Text color
- Text size
- Font
- Text opacity
- Text background color
- Edge style
- Window background color
- Text background opacity
- Reset defaults
- Window background opacity
- Reset defaults

Calling and Messaging Without Speech

With Calling and Messaging without Speech allows you to see transcripts of your messages. To enable this feature, do the following:

1. Swipe down from the top of the screen and then select Settings.
2. Tap on Accessibility
3. After that you should select Calling & Messaging Without Speech
4. You can then toggle this feature on or off.

Using the VoiceView Screen Reader

You can have Alexa read the words displayed on your Echo Show screen. When this feature is enabled you can also use gestures to navigate through your Echo Show's menu. VoiceView can also describe the actions that you are making as you go along.

There are a couple of ways so you can enable this feature. They are the following:

Method #1

1. Press the mic/camera button and hold it down – this is one of the three buttons at the top of your Echo Show (i.e. the first one from left to right when you are facing the screen).
2. When you hold it down for a few seconds an alert will sound. After that touch the screen with two fingers (keep fingers apart) and keep them on the screen for 5 seconds.

Method #2

1. Swipe downward from the top of the screen using three fingers
2. Select accessibility

3. Select VoiceView Screen Reader
4. Select VoiceView

VoiceView User Settings

To access the settings of the VoiceView function, swipe downward from the top of your Echo Show's screen using three fingers. Tap on Settings and then go to Accessibility and then double tap on VoiceView Screen Reader. The available settings will then be displayed on screen.

Here are the settings that you can adjust:

- *Reading Speed* – adjusts the speed of the speech
- *Speech Volume* – adjusts the volume level of the reading voice. You can also adjust it to Match Device Volume so that it uses the same volume settings for your movies and other videos.
- *Sound Volume* – adjusts the volume of feedback tones. You can also set this to Match Device Volume.
- *Key Echo* – the default setting is to echo the characters you type as you enter them. That can get annoying sometimes; if that is the case then you can just set it to none (no echoing of the characters you type), characters (default setting), words (only entire words are echoed or read back to you), and characters and words (all characters and all words will be read back to you as you type them).
- *Punctuation Level* – you set which punctuations are read back to you.

VoiceView Gestures

The following are gestures that can be used to explore your Amazon Echo.

- Turn VoiceView On/Off from Anywhere

Press the Mic/Camera button until the alert sounds. After the alert press two fingers against the screen for five seconds.

- Display the status bar to gain access to Accessibility settings on the Echo Show

To do that, swipe downward from the top of the Amazon Echo Show screen using three fingers.

- Moving to the next page on the screen or the previous page

In order to move to the next page on the screen, swipe to the right using three fingers. To see the previous page, swipe to the left using three fingers.

- Read items on the screen

To have Alexa read the different screen items, drag your finger over the items that you want Alexa to read them to you.

- Have Alexa read the next item on the screen

To make Alexa read the next screen item swipe the screen going to the right with one finger.

- Go to a previous screen item

To make Alexa read back a previous item swipe with one finger going to the left

- Open a screen item

To open an item on the screen place and hold a finger on an item briefly (just about a second) so as to focus on that item (if you

68

have your screen reader turned on it will read that item for you). After the focus (which is just exactly the same amount of time your screen reader can read that item) double tap on that item to launch or open it.

- Increase granularity

Increasing the granularity of screen items makes it easier to have Alexa spell words out. To increase granularity swipe up and down on the screen in one single stroke or motion using only one finger.

- Decrease granularity

To decrease screen granularity, swipe up and down on the screen with one finger in one continuous motion.

- Typing on the onscreen keyboard

To type on your Echo Show's onscreen keyboard swipe across the letters using one finger. Alexa will read each letter out loud to you. When your finger lands on the letter you wish to type (i.e. when your finger lands on the exact letter you want to type) then lift your finger from off the screen or keyboard and then the letter will be entered.

- Scrolling up or down

To scroll through a list of items, use three fingers to swipe up or down to scroll through the list.

- Scrolling from left to right

When scrolling is available from left to right (Alexa will inform you) scroll with thre fingers going either to the left or to the right to scroll through the different items on the list.

- Stop speech

To stop Alexa from reading stuff on your Amazon Echo Show's screen, do a single tap on the screen using two fingers.

- Read everything from items you select

To have Alexa read everything from items you select, swipe downward using two of your fingers starting with the item you want Alexa to read from off the screen.

- Have Alexa read everything from the very first item

If you want Alexa to read everything instead of reading a selection of items, swipe upward using only two fingers.

- Start or stop any media from playing

To start or stop your Echo Show from playing media just double tap on the screen using two fingers.

- Mute and unmute speech

To have Alexa mute or unmute her reading speech double tap anywhere on the Echo Show screen using three fingers.

- Modify settings on slider controls

Slider controls are used to adjust settings on your Amazon Echo Show. Settings like volume, brightness, and others are adjusted using these controls. To adjust these slider controls using your gesture controls simply place focus on the slider you want to adjust and then move the slide either to the left or to the right to decrease or increase its setting.

- Enter or exit the Echo Show's Learn Mode

Learn Mode is a module that you can use to practice swiping, placing focus, and other gesture controls on your Echo Show. It's a great way for you to learn all the gesture controls that are available. To activate Learn Mode double tap on the screen using four fingers. To deactivate Learn Mode double tap on the screen again using four fingers.

- Make the reader start with the first item on the screen

To do this tap the upper half of your Echo Show screen using four fingers

- Go to the last on screen item

To do this, tap the Echo Screen's lower half

Chapter 11: Restrict Access to Echo Show

It makes sense to restrict access to your Echo Show. You don't just anybody to have access to your Amazon Prime privileges, right? You can also use restrictions as a form of parental control – you don't' want to have your kids watching inappropriate material through your Echo Show when you're not around.

Here are some of the features that can be set with restrictions:

- Web Videos – both search and playback options to web videos can be restricted. On top of that you can also implement the Echo Show's Safe Search mode. This is a type of parental control, which blocks material or content that are mature or otherwise inappropriate for children.
- Movie Trailers – enabling restriction settings will also block access to movie trailers.
- Prime Photos – restrictions can also be placed on viewing your Prime Photos and albums. This setting also restricts access to the Photo Booth feature. It also prevents other people from changing your Amazon Echo Show's background screen.

Since we already mentioned the Safe Search mode, it should be noted that the restrictions only apply to voice searches. There are no restrictions applied if the search was made through the Echo Show's on screen keyboard.

Setting Up Restrictions on Your Echo Show

Here's how you set restrictions on your device

1. Swipe downward from the top of the screen and then select Settings.
2. Alternatively you can just say "Alexa (or your preferred wake word), go to settings."
3. Select any of the features mentioned above that you want to restrict access to.
4. Follow the on screen prompts to have that feature restricted.

Okay, so some of you may also want to restrict access to Prime Videos through the Amazon Echo Show (or other Alexa enabled device). However, you can't do that specifically just for your Echo Show, Amazon Echo, Echo Dot, Echo Spot or whatever Echo device Amazon may introduce next.

To disable or restrict access to Prime Videos in your account you need to log on to your Amazon Prime account through your browser and then go to Prime Video Settings. From there you can restrict access to Prime Videos.

Chapter 12: Alexa Skills for the Echo Show

Currently there are two Amazon Alexa products that also feature a touch screen – the Amazon Echo Show and the Echo Spot. This is a new and unique feature that gives the good old Echo speakers a visual upgrade. You can say that it adds a new dimension to what smart assistants can do for you.

With the coming of this new feature for Echo devices everywhere in the world, comes the influx of new skills that now apply to an Echo device that has a touch screen. We'll only cover the skills that are compatible with the Echo Show in this chapter although some of these skills can also work with the Echo Spot, well this book is about the Echo anyway.

Fandango Skill

This skill was published in October 3, 2017 and it is a pretty good skill. Of course it tackles a fairly difficult task – finding information about nearby movies that you can watch. It's a pretty good skill to add to your Amazon Echo Show; imagine having Alexa get you inside info on a spur of the moment movie night (or even a scheduled one at that).

When this skill was first launched the big hang up about it was its inability to repeat the movie info and listings. You had to repeat the whole shebang all over again just to get to that movie and show time that you were interested in.

Well, that was before when Alexa only had voice capabilities. Now, with the Amazon Echo Show, this skill has taken things up a notch. You can hear Alexa tell you which movies are on and their play times but on top of that you have all the listings displayed on your Echo Show screen.

The other cool thing about Fandango is that you can buy the movie tickets through this skill. Look for a movie that you like, checkout the show times, and then buy tickets. The downside of this skill is the fact that you need a Fandango VIP account in order for you to buy tickets online via this skill.

Best features:

- It is free to enable
- "Alexa, open Fandango"
- "Alexa, I want to buy some movie tickets" (no need to invoke the keyword "Fandango")
- "The second one" (Alexa can clarify which movie you want to watch and you can interact as if you were talking to her directly).
- You can purchase movie tickets through the app as long as you have a Fandango VIP account.
- Allows users to see movie listings on the Echo Show's screen. You can also buy tickets through the touch screen as well.

You can get this skill here:

https://www.amazon.com/Fandango-Inc/dp/B01N5FH66U

Twitch Skill

Alright, so we already mentioned in an earlier chapter (or actually several times in this book now so you will remember that fact) that you can't watch YouTube videos anymore on your Amazone Echo Show.

Well, the two companies kind of had some sort of reconciliation back in November 2017 just before Black Friday but you can say that negotiations broke down and Google complained about Amazon's unwillingness to reciprocate their efforts – or some such details.

Well, anyway, there are other things that you can watch other than YouTube videos anyway. And that is where Twitch comes in for the quick save – talk about deus ex machina.

Well, there is a huge market for gamers in today's digital age. On top of that there are lots of people who would rather prefer to watch other gamers play (especially the really good ones). They even find that more entertaining than watching a movie.

For instance, there were plenty of epic moments in the game Fortnite and who knows which one you'll catch up to when you get to watch it happen with the Twitch skill. In addition to the usual stuff that you can do with a skill like this (e.g. get announcements about your favorite streams coming up, discover new streamers, etc.) you now get to watch the streams on your Echo Show.

On top of that you will also be joining a community of millions (current count is at 10 million and rising) who watch games and talk about games and really epic gamers. In the case of Twitch, you also get to enjoy the company of people who are into creative arts and music since these are also a huge part of any gaming environment.

Features and Commands:

- Get notifications about your favorite channels

- Know which channels are streaming
- Alexa suggests which games are currently trending, which basically helps you discover new games that can become your favorite.
- "Alexa, open Twitch" (activates the Twitch skill)
- "Alexa, ask Twitch for followed channels"
- "Alexa, tell Twitch to show me channels I follow"
- "Alexa, ask Twitch to suggest an IRL channel"
- "Alexa, ask Twitch to play [say channel name]" (plays the specified channel)

NOTE: don't forget to enable the notification permissions for the Twitch skill so Alexa can send you notifications.

Twitch is free to enable and you can do that here:

https://www.amazon.com/Amazon-Twitch/dp/B076C836XS

Allrecipes Cooking Skill

When it comes to the myriad of digital food brands in the market today Allrecipes is definitely one of the biggest if not the biggest one out there. They boast of a total of more than 80 million users (and that number is growing by the way).

How many visits do they get each year? They have a total of 1.5 billion unique annual visits. Of course, when Amazon released the very first Amazon Echo, Allrecipes was one of the first brands to hop in the bandwagon.

They were one of the earliest to include cooking content that capitalizes on voice activation. The original skill they launched back then was specifically designed for the Amazon Echo and also the Echo Dot. Obviously all the cooking content they provided was audio.

However, with the introduction of the Amazon Echo Show and Echo Spot things had to change a bit. Well, it's one thing to listen to someone tell you how to cook your next culinary masterpiece and it's another to have someone actually show it to you.

Besides, food also tends to be visually stimulating. Seeing how good your dish should look like will help encourage would-be culinary masters (or at least accomplished home cooks).

The all new revamped Allrecipes Alexa skill will include access to a database of 60,000 recipes. Apart from the recipes, the skill now walks you through the preparation and actually cooking process. Now that is a really massive database at your fingertips... or video screen to be exact.

Now, there is a downside to this – so hang on to your seats. It's a massive database right? It is a two-edged sword, it is the skill's strength and it is also its weakness. Sometimes Alexa has trouble finding a particular recipe even if you included it as one of your favorites – if that happens you just have to keep asking Alexa to try and find your recipe and she will eventually find it. Oh well, we can always hope things to improve in the next update.

Features and Commands:

- Alexa, open Allrecipes (launches the skill)
- Alexa, ask Allrecipes what can I cook with [mention ingredients]
- Alexa, ask Allrecipes for the recipe of the day.
- What ingredients do I need to make this recipe
- Tell me the review about this recipe
- Alexa, send this recipe to my phone
- Alexa, next step (when you want to know the next step in the cooking instructions)

You can get the Allrecipes skill here:

https://www.amazon.com/Allrecipes/dp/B01N3MS7AV

CNN Skill

You can get flash briefings straight from CNN with this skill

Features and commands:

- Alexa, open CNN
- Alexa, ask CNN for the latest news
- Alexa, ask CNN for a binge

Enable the CNN skill here:

https://www.amazon.com/CNN-Interactive-Group-Inc/dp/B01LX24O05

Nest Camera Skill

This skill of course works best with the Nest Camera. It allows you to view the cameras footage right on your Amazon Echo Show screen.

Features and commands:

- Alexa, show the front door
- Alexa, show the feed from the backyard
- Alexa, hide the kids room

Enable this skill here:

https://www.amazon.com/Nest-Labs-Inc-Camera/dp/B072KV8NJ5

Chapter 13: Troubleshooting Issues

In a perfect world, everything should work just as planned. But we all know that this is not a perfect world so we need to try and fix things when things do go wrong. Can things go wrong for the Echo Show? The answer is yes.

We'll go over some issues that people experience with their Echo Show and the troubleshooting steps that can be used to fix them.

Echo Show Won't Power On

- Faulty Power Adapter

Check for a faulty power adapter. Make sure that the power adapter is plugged in. Pull it out of the wall and check for damage. Check the other end of the power adapter (the one that goes into the back of the Echo Show) and see if it has any damage.

Plug the power adapter to a different wall outlet. If the Echo Show still won't power on consider replacing the power adapter. Call Amazon tech support for other possible options and to get a replacement adapter if your product is still under warranty.

- Faulty Motherboard

The good news is that unlike your computer, the Echo Show has fewer parts. In case the new power adapter still doesn't solve this issue then your Show's motherboard will need a replacement. Call Amazon for replacement parts and to make a warranty claim.

Echo Show's Screen is Frozen

So what do you do if your Echo Show screen is unresponsive? You tap, swipe, and nothing happens. There are three possible trouble points when this happens:

- A dirty screen – it could all be nothing than a dirty screen. The current technology used for the Amazon Echo Show screen makes use of infrared LED lights. If there are any particles on the screen that block the light then that can cause a problem. Use a screen cleaner and a soft cloth to clean the screen all the way to the edges.
- It just needs a reboot – sometimes all your electronics need is a restart. Turn off your Echo Show, wait for 10 seconds and then turn it back on.
- Faulty LED Circuit Board – call this the worst case scenario. You've given the screen a good wipe down and you have restarted your Echo Show and still the screen isn't responding. Better call it in and let Amazon's tech support guys do the work and get you a replacement.

Buttons Not Working or are Missing

Another issue or problem that can occur with the Amazon Echo Show is that the button may not be responding or working. In some instances, when a brand new unit is delivered to your door, a button or two is missing.

If you have missing buttons on your new Alexa device then you should contact customer support and arrange to get a replacement. However, in the case of faulty buttons you should try cleaning them first with a clean cloth and then restart your Echo Show. If that doesn't solve the problem then call customer support.

Echo Show Can't Connect to the Internet/Wireless Network

One issue that people have reported about their Echo Show is that it can't connect to their wireless network at home or it can connect to WiFi but can't connect to the Internet.

Some technical specs that you should remember, and this you can check out on your router, is that your Show can connect to 802.11a / b / g / n networks. They also do not connect to peer to peer networks. Simply put, your Echo Show should connect directly to the router.

Your first indication that your Echo Show isn't connecting to your wireless network is when the display indicator is colored orange – you'll see a orange (-ish) sort of line at the bottom of the Echo Show's screen. That means it isn't connected to a Wi-Fi network.

Here are some troubleshooting steps that you can try:

- **Wi-Fi Connection is on Snooze Mode:** Maybe your Echo Show's Wi-Fi is disabled. Go to settings and if your device's Wi-Fi settings is enabled or is not in snooze mode. If it is, then reset your WiFi settings and scan for available networks.

- **Give Everything a Fresh Start:** Here's a good way to get things fixed– restart everything. Let's give your router and Echo Show a fresh start. Maybe they just need some time out before they can get together – pun intended there.

  But seriously yes, you should first turn off your router and then restart it and that goes the same for your Echo Show. Usually that fixes a lot of wireless networking problems. This can work for your phone or other devices too.

Just remember to power off your router and then wait for 10 seconds and then power it back on. Do the same for your Echo Show – power off and then wait for ten seconds then plug the power cord back on.

- **Rescan and Search for Available Wi-Fi Networks:** Another thing that you can do (that is if restarting doesn't work or if you're in a rush and don't want to restart your equipment) is to make your Echo Show scan for wireless networks again. To do that swipe down from the top of the screen and then you need to go to Settings and then tap WiFi. Your Echo Show will scan for available networks. If you see your wireless network on the screen then it's good news. Select that network and login.

- **Use Other Devices to Connect:** Another thing you can do is to check if other devices like your phone, tablet, or computer can connect to your wireless network. If other devices can't connect to your Wi-Fi then you need to reconfigure your router and/or modem. If your wireless devices including your Echo Show can connect to the wireless network but still can't connect to the internet then you need to contact your Internet Service Provider.

- **Reduce Wireless Congestion:** Sometimes there are interferences in the wireless signal being broadcast by your router. Reposition your Echo Show and move it away from baby monitors and microwave ovens. You should also keep it away from the wall – at least 8 inches off the wall.

If your Amazon Echo Show is in a room or some area that is far away from the router or if there is a wall blocking it off, then move it closer to the router.

Now, you may be using too many wireless devices in your home. Turn off some of the other wireless devices for the mean time. Test if your Echo Show can connect online by playing music or video from via your Amazon account.

If your wireless network is congested you should adjust your configuration. Note that a lot of wireless devices use the 2.5 GHz band. Switch to the 5 GHz band to reduce the congestion in your wireless network.

I Forgot My Wi-Fi Password

Sometimes people forget their password for pretty much everything. We have set our devices to remember everything so you don't have to worry about it, right? Unfortunately, if you failed to save your wireless network password to Amazon and you buy a new Echo device, then you will really need to enter the password when you login your new device. This can happen if you are adding a new Amazon Echo Show to your network.

The good news is that there are a few things that you can try that may save the day. Here they are:

- Check the bottom of your router. There is usually a sticker there that tells you what the SSID is (i.e. the network name) and the passphrase or key (i.e. your wireless network's password).
- Another thing you can try is to go over your router's user's manual or owner's guide. Sometimes they have router's password printed there.
- Another thing that you can try is to use a computer that is already connected to your Wi-Fi. See the instructions below:

How to use your computer to figure out your wireless network's password? Let's start with Windows (i.e. Windows 10) users first:

1. On your desktop, right click the wireless network icon. It should be right next to the clock and calendar on the lower right corner of the screen. Click on "Open Network and Sharing Center."
2. In the section that says "View your active networks" click on the name of your wireless network. It should be on the right under Access Type and it would usually say "Wi-Fi(<your wireless network name>)"

3. After clicking on that, the Wi-Fi Status window will pop up. Under **Connection**, click on Wireless Properties or just press Alt+W.
4. The Wireless Connection Properties window will then pop up. Now, click on the **Security** tab.
5. Now, click on the box that says "Show characters"
6. After doing that you will see your *wireless network's password* in the Network Security Key box.

Now, here's how you do that in Mac OS X:

1. Open the Utilities folder.
2. Click the Keychain Access app.
3. Select the name of your wireless network.
4. Click on the Info button.
5. Check the box at that part that says Show Password.
6. You will be asked to enter the administrator password – enter that and then you will see your Wi-Fi password listed.

Note that if all of that didn't work then you will have to reconfigure your router's wireless network. You may have to ask the assistance of the person who configured your Wi-Fi the last time.

There are Lines or Dead Pixels on My Echo Show Screen

Nope, that is not a new skill or an update. If there are visible lines or dead pixels on your Echo Show screen then there is definitely something wrong. Here's what you can do:

1. Check for interferences – believe it or not other devices can interfere with your Amazon Echo Show. Moving it away from other appliances like a printer, computer, microwave,

and others can sometimes do the trick. After repositioning your Echo Show, you should power cycle your device.

2. Faulty Echo Show screen –if the lines are still there are your restart and repositioning then it could be a faulty screen. You should call Amazon's customer support and get a replacement.

Chapter 14: Resetting Your Amazon Echo Show

What do you mean by resetting my Amazon Echo Show? A reset simply means starting over and setting up your Echo Show as if it came right out of the box all over again. In other words, it's a factory reset.

Why Do a Reset?

Why would you want to do that with this device? There are times when this is your only course of action – that means you're already out of options. Let's say your Echo Show is stuck on a screen or mode and it is no longer responding to the touch screen controls or to your voice commands.

Some might think that maybe a restart is all it needs. Well, sometimes even after how many times you restart an Echo device or other devices and pieces of electronics, sometimes it still doesn't work. You know what; this happens to computers too you know.

You've tried everything and boom, it still doesn't work like it used to. For your computer, you reformat the thing but for devices like the Echo Show (and your phone too by the way), that is the equivalent of a factory reset.

You would also want to reset your Amazon Echo Show in case you want to give it away to someone else as a gift or something. Well, you may have a lot of data and other stuff in there. Erasing all the data and then messing around with the settings to get them all back to the original will take a lot of time – and who's got the time to do all that confusing stuff, right?

How to Do a Device Reset

A device reset is fairly easy enough to do and the process should take only a few minutes. In case you think that a device reset is what you need to resolve an issue with your Amazon Echo Show then we advise that you restart your device first before you do a reset.

To restart your Echo Show, all you need to do is unplug the power cable at the back or just unplug the cable from the power outlet instead. Wait for 10 seconds and then plug it back again. If that still doesn't resolve the issue you are experiencing with your device then it's time for a reset.

Here are the steps you need to perform to do a factory reset on your Amazon Echo Show:

1. Swipe from the top of the screen going down. And then you should select Settings.
2. In settings go to Device Options.
3. After that tap on Reset to Factory Defaults.
4. Note that when you select that your Echo Show will start to erase all your personal information including the settings that you have made on this device. After the device resets it will commence with the set up process. That means you will need to do everything all over again.
5. You will be prompted to connect to your Wi-Fi network, download updates (which will again take a good deal of time), and all the other stuff.

Consider this as your last resort to resolve any problems that you may have with the overall functionality of your Amazon Echo Show. If this still doesn't resolve the problem then you will have to call customer support and report the problem. If your product is within warranty then you may be able to get a replacement of your Echo Show.

Chapter 15: Quick Reference Section

How to Do Things with the Echo Show

In this chapter we have consolidated the most common things you can do with your Echo show. Since we have covered these things in the previous chapters we won't describe them in detail. We'll just show you how to do them. The steps here usually outline how to turn a feature on or off. Some of the instructions here will just show you how to use a particular function.

Power Cycle the Echo Show

Unplug your device from the wall and then wait for 10 seconds. After that you should turn on your device by plugging it into the wall.

Change Wake Word via the Alexa App

To change the wake word via the Alexa app, turn on your mobile device or computer. First off, you should tap the hamburger button (you can skip this step if you are doing this on your computer's browser. After that, tap on Settings, select the Echo Show in your list of devices (you'll see all of your Echo devices listed), next scroll down to wake word, after that select your wake word from the list, and then finally select *Save*.

Change Wake Word via Voice Command

If you don't want to use your phone or the Alexa App to change the wake word, then you can try changing it by simply talking to Alexa. Remember that the for the Amazon Echo Show, the default wake word is "Alexa."

To change it to the other options available you should first call your Echo Show's attention by saying "Alexa" (or if you have changed it to something else then use that wake word instead).

After that use the following command *"Go to settings."* After that, tell Alexa to go to Device Settings, and then to Wake Word. After that choose the **new wake word** you prefer to use.

Okay, that's the long version. Here's how you do it real quick with one command:

- Say the current wake word
- And then say "change your wake word to..."
- And then say the new wake word you want to use.

After that Alexa will tell you that you can call her using the new wake word in a few seconds. Now, if you forgot the wake words that you can use then you just ask her the following:

"Alexa (or any other current wake word you're using) what are your wake words?"

Alexa will first ask you if you want to change the current wake word and then she will tell you what current wake words you can use as a replacement. You will then be asked which one do you like in case you opted at that time to change the current wake word.

Alternatively you can ask her "Alexa, can we change your name?" and then she will give you options to change to.

Change the Wake Word via the Touch Screen

If you don't like going through the voice prompts when talking to Alexa or you don't want to mess with the settings on the Amazon App then a third option for you is to change it through the Echo Show's touch screen – some people find it easier to change settings here too.

Here's how you can do that:

- On your Amazon Echo Show screen, swipe from the top going downwards.
- From the screen that pulls up, tap on Device Options or Options
- After that tap on Wake Word
- Then select the wake word you would like to use
- Tap save

Note that when you change the wake word your Echo Show's visual indicator or home screen will briefly flash to an orange color and then back to blue. Now you can test if Alexa responds to the new wake word by issuing other commands or asking questions.

Connecting Your Echo Show to a Wireless Network

As stated in an earlier chapter, you need an active wireless network to make the most out of your Echo Show. One of the first things that you will do upon initial setup is to connect to your device to WiFi.

There are several ways to do that. The first way is via the touch screen on the Echo Show itself. Here are the steps:

1. Plug your Echo Show to the wall if it is not powered on
2. Swipe downward from the top screen and tap Settings. Alternatively you can say "Alexa, go to settings."
3. In the Settings menu tap WiFi
4. Echo Show will then scan for available wireless networks. Select your WiFi in the list.
5. You will be prompted to enter your WiFi password – enter that and follow the other prompts when they come up.
6. Finally, tap Connect and your Echo Show will connect to that wireless network.

What if you don't see your wireless network listed? Follow these steps:

1. Swipe down on the screen and go to Settings > WiFi
2. Scroll down to the bottom of the page to add your wireless network. You will be required to enter the necessary credentials such as your WiFi network's SSID (or network name) and the password. You will also find other advanced wireless connection options in that section of the menu.

Here's how you connect your Echo Show to a wireless network via the Alexa App:

1. Open the Alexa App.
2. Go to Menu > Alexa Devices
3. In the list of devices tap Amazon Echo Show. Note that if you already have other devices in the list and you haven't

added your Show to the list, then tap/click **Add Alexa Device** and follow the prompts to add your Echo Show.

4. Select "Change" from Wi-Fi Network (it's right beside it). Your Echo Show will then scan for available wireless networks.

5. Select your wireless network in the list and then enter the password for that network.

6. If your wireless network isn't displayed then tap Rescan. If that doesn't work then tap/click Add a Network and then follow the same steps above about adding a wireless network.

7. Some WiFi networks are setup with a Mac filter. To find your Echo Show's Mac Filter, open your Alexa App and go to the menu and then Alexa Devices. Select your Echo Show on the list and then scroll down and then you should tap "About." You will find your device's Mac Filter there and you can add that to your router's configuration.

8. Finally, tap Connect and your Echo Show will connect to that wireless network.

Saving Your WiFi Password on Amazon's Servers

If you are planning to add more Echo devices to your home, then it makes sense to save your wireless network password online so that when you add a new Echo device you won't have to repeat the same process of registering your new device to your WiFi connection.

This is also convenient in case you usually switch from one wireless network to the other – the password is remembered so you don't have to enter it each time you switch to a different network. When you setup the wireless connectivity of your Echo Show you will be asked if you want the password to be saved to Amazon. It's up to you if you want to choose that option or not at this point.

Connecting to Public Networks

Follow the same steps outlined in the section for connecting to a WiFi network. You may be required to enter certain credentials such as the network's SSID, your Echo Show's Mac address, and the WiFi password which should be provided to you by the owner of the network.

Public networks can be found in a library, cafes, and other stores. Note that the passwords for these public networks can't be saved to Amazon.

Reset Amazon Echo Show

1. Swipe from the top of the screen going down. And then you should select Settings.
2. In settings go to Device Options.
3. After that tap on Reset to Factory Defaults.

Adjust Screen Brightness

1. Slide downwards from the top of the screen
2. You will see the brightness setting with a slider on the top right side of the menu.
3. Move the slider up and down to adjust screen brightness.

Toggle Adaptive Brightness

You can let your Echo Show adjust the screen brightness automatically or you can just turn this feature off if you want to. Here's how:

1. Go to Settings
2. Scroll down to Display
3. Scroll down again until you find Adaptive Brightness
4. Toggle it on or off.

Adjust Volume Levels

You can use the volume buttons at the top of the Echo Show to adjust volume levels. Other than that you can also use the following voice commands:

- Alexa, louder – turns up the volume one level higher.
- Alexa, softer – turns down the current volume level one step lower.

- Alexa, set volume to [mention any number from 0 to 10] – sets the volume to a level you specify.
- Alexa, mute – Echo Show sounds are muted.
- Alexa, unmute – Echo Show sounds are unmuted.

Adjust Scheduled Alarm Volume

You can adjust the volume of your timer or alarm by going to settings. Here's how you can do that:

1. Say "Alexa, go to settings" or just swipe downward from the top of the screen and then tap on Settings.
2. Scroll down to Sounds in the next screen
3. Next, scroll down to Alarm, Timer, and Notification Volume
4. Move the slider underneath this setting to adjust your timer/alarm volume

Conclusion

I hope this book was able to help you to learn all about the Amazon Echo Show. It's a really useful tool and its accessibility features along with the rest of its functions can be big help in the home. If you already have Alexa in the house then the Echo Show is a welcome addition and a really good upgrade.

It has its downsides of course but upgrades are still underway. We can expect Alexa to improve and so with the capabilities of the Echo Show. Who knows maybe the guys from Amazon would also decide to bring down the price.

I wish you the best of luck!

To your success,

William Seals

www.ingramcontent.com/pod-product-compliance
Lightning Source LLC
LaVergne TN
LVHW092030060326
832903LV00058B/499